LOVE IS ALWAYS!

# Love is Always!

## *A Positive Affirmation Book for Kids*

## CASSANDRA CRUZ-DOCKERY & NADINE ANTOINE-MUSANGI

*Sarai Foster*

Blooming Pages LLC

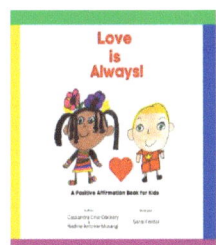

Love is Always!

I love my life! Aiden

I love being me! Maddie

I have all I need to succeed! Jonah

I am loved. Autumn

I am kind. Janae

I am a great friend to others! Danny

I can do great things! Stacey

I am filled with love. Lucy

I am a gift to my family! Juan Pablo

I am creative! Kiki

I am worthy of love! Eddie

I am unique! Keisha

I am amazing! Zuri

I love my skin! Kiki Danny

I am loved by many. 

Love is always! Penny

# Dedications

To all the Blooming Scholars, know that YOU are
ALWAYS seen, heard & LOVED!
Blooming Pages

To my mom, family, and Ms. Cruz. Thank you for
encouraging, loving, and supporting me!
Sarai Foster

# BLOOMING PAGES
## Rooted in Learning

July 2, 2023
ISBN# 979-8-9875905-5-3

# Love
# is
# Always!

## A Positive Affirmation Book for Kids

Authors

**Cassandra Cruz-Dockery**
**&**
**Nadine Antoine-Musangi**

Illustrator

**Sarai Foster**

# I love my life!

Aiden

# I love being me!

Maddie

# I have all I need to succeed! ❤️

Jonah

# I am loved.

Autumn

# I am kind.

Janae

# I am a great friend to others!

Danny

# I can do great things!

Stacey

# I am filled with love.

Lucy

# I am a gift to my family!

Juan Pablo

# I am creative!

Kiki

# I am worthy of love!

Eddie

# I am unique!

Keisha

# I am amazing!

Zuri

# I love my skin!

Kiki

Danny

# I am loved by many.

# Love is always!

Penny

**Touch a heart as you say each affirmation out loud.**

♥ I love my life.

♥ I love being me.

♥ I have all I need to succeed.

♥ I am loved.

♥ I am kind.

♥ I love my skin.

♥ I can do great things.

♥ I am creative!

BLOOMING PAGES
Rooted in Learning

**Touch a heart as you say each affirmation out loud.**

💗 I am a great friend to others!

💗 I am a gift to my family!

💗 I am worthy of love.

💗 I am unique.

💗 I am amazing.

💗 I am filled with love.

💗 I am loved by many.

💗 Love is always!

BLOOMING PAGES
**Rooted in Learning**

# Draw Yourself

# Write your own affirmation(s)

## BLOOMING PAGES
### Rooted in Learning

**Visit us today!**

Blooming Pages is a small business founded by two Teacher Moms who want to continue supporting teachers, parents, and young children beyond the classroom. Our mission is to support, empower and guide teachers and parents on ways to help their children build a solid academic foundation from the very beginning. Blooming Pages provides engaging and interactive teacher and parent classes, workshops, and resources that lead children in becoming confident learners, independent thinkers, and all-around Blooming Scholars. To learn more, visit us at www.Bloomingpages.info

## We work with...

Early Childhood Educators
Parents of children aged
3-8 years old
PTA/SAC
School Administrators
and Coaches
Afterschool programs

## We provide

Primary Teacher Professional
Development Parent Development
Workshops
Family Engagment Workshops
Kid-Friendly Activity
Classes
Kindergarten Readiness
Classes
Story Time Events
Coaching & Consultations Activities
and Resources for Pre-K,
Kindergarten, 1st & 2nd Graders

# Our Story

## Blooming Pages- Authors

Cassandra and Nadine met Sarai in 2022 when she was a student in Mrs. Cruz's (Cassandra) Kindergarten classroom and Mrs. Antoine (Nadine) was the literacy coach at the same school.

They were able to see that Sarai had a positive spirit and a special talent. She had to ability to put her thoughts on paper and share her skills with her peers. She has the ability to capture the essence of each character that she drew. She created each one to stand out, just like the way children do!

At the end of the year, we began adding life to her beautiful illustrations by adding positive affirmations to each character.
We hope you can find one that resonates with your inner child.
"When we work together, we grow together"

@Bloomingpages.info

## Sarai Foster- Illustrator

Sarai Foster is currently a second-grade student at Rock Island Elementary School. When she grows up, Sarai is hoping to pursue her dream of becoming a teacher.
During Sarai's free time, she enjoys playing video games, drawing, and playing with her toys. She enjoys drawing pictures because she loves art and hopes to teach it someday. Sarai's passion for art is evident in her work and will continue to improve over the years.